From BUDLEIGH SALTERTON ...With Love

GEORGE PRIDMORE

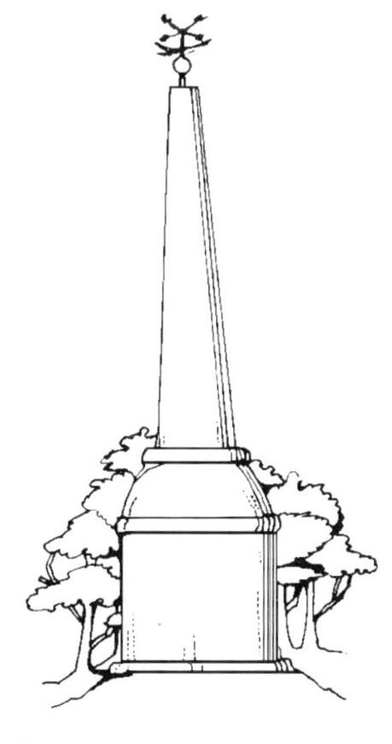

OBELISK PUBLICATIONS

Also by the Author:

Wish You Were Here … at Exmouth
From Exmouth … With Love

Some Other Titles of Interest from Obelisk Publications:

From Teignmouth … With love, Viv Wilson
Adventure Through Red Devon, Raymond B. Cattell
ExtraOrdinary Exmouth, Harry Pascoe
Talking About Topsham, Sara Vernon
Dawlish and Dawlish Warren, Chips Barber
Ten Family Walks in East Devon, Sally and Chips Barber
TV and Films Made in Devon, Chips Barber and David FitzGerald
Around & About Seaton and Beer, Chips Barber
Around & About Sidmouth, Chips Barber
Around and About Teignmouth and Shaldon, Chips Barber
Tales of the Unexplained in Devon, Judy Chard
Haunted Happenings in Devon, Judy Chard
The Lost City of Exeter, Chips Barber
The Great Little Exeter Book, Chips Barber
The Ghosts of Exeter, Sally and Chips Barber
Ghastly and Ghostly Devon, Sally and Chips Barber
Ian Jubb's *Exeter Collection*
Beautiful Exeter, Chips Barber
More…Cobblestones, Cottages and Castles, David Young
The A to Z of Villages, David Young

Obelisk Publications specialise in books about Devon topics and themes. If you would like further details of currently available titles, please send an s.a.e. to the address given below or telephone (0392) 468556.

This book is dedicated to my four children, two of whom were born in Budleigh Salterton.

First published in 1993 by
Obelisk Publications, 2 Church Hill, Pinhoe, Exeter, Devon
Designed by Chips and Sally Barber
Typeset by Sally Barber
Printed in Great Britain
by Maslands Limited, Tiverton, Devon.

From BUDLEIGH SALTERTON *...With Love*

It is a tradition, when on holiday, to send picture postcards to relatives, friends, work colleagues and neighbours, telling them about the journey, weather, accommodation, food and holiday activities.

They may carry familiar phrases like 'Having a good time', 'Wish you were here' or 'With love', to assure those left behind that they are not forgotten. But picture postcards have been used for other purposes, such as conveying seasonal greetings; advertising a trade or business; providing a memory of an event; or simply sending a message.

This book contains a selection of cards sent from the Budleigh Salterton area in the earlier part of this century and provides a record of social history, showing the change in appearances and attitudes over the years.

GREETINGS FROM BUDLEIGH SALTERTON

Here we have three views of Budleigh Salterton's High Street. The place where many of the postcards started their journeys was at Budleigh Salterton Post Office, on the corner of High Street and The Lawn. In the above picture a cyclist can be seen pedalling up the High Street on the wrong side but quite safely as there was precious little traffic to pose any problems.

The top picture on the opposite page carried birthday greetings in 1907, through the post, to a lady in nearby Otterton … from South Lambeth in London!

The bottom picture opposite shows the junction of High Street and Fore Street when a bank occupied the Chapel Street corner site. Also visible are the thriving businesses of 'Bennett – ironmonger, plumber, gasfitter, sanitary engineer and house agent'; 'Barns Restaurant' and 'Cowd's Haircutting & Shampooing Saloon, Tobacconist'.

Budleigh Salterton. High Street.

Budleigh Salterton, High Street.

At Otterton Village

Budleigh Salterton.
Fore Street.

Whoops! The top picture on the opposite page has made a very obvious mistake. Anyone who knows their East Devon will instantly recognize this picture as Budleigh Salterton and not Otterton as stated on the card. This particular view was sent to wish a friend a 'Happy New Year' for 1908. Despite the passing of more than four score years this scene is still easily identifiable with the brook babbling its way seawards, as it still does today!

The bottom photograph opposite looks the other way up Fore Street. One can almost imagine the police sergeant asking the man, "Excuse me Sir, are you the owner of that contraption across the road...?"

Above is the Marine Hotel, which was situated across the road from the Methodist Church. This card was sent from there in 1914. The hotel, originally The Coffee House, was a temperance establishment. It no longer exists as it was demolished.

In the 1930s hotel proprietors realized that a good way of publicizing their establishments (and their proximity to the sea) was to use postcards showing aerial views. Many hotels latched on to this and this photo is just one of a

number that appeared at that time. The large hotel in the centre of the picture was The Rolle Hotel, which took its name from a famous family in East Devon. Unfortunately the golden age of hotels for Salterton has gone.

Another hotel that has been demolished is The Rosemullion, in its hey day one of the top hotels in East Devon. It was demolished in the 1980s and today is the site of flats.

The caption on the top photo opposite clearly says Westboro' Terrace but is, in fact, Westbourne Terrace, off West Hill as it looked in 1911 when the card was sent.

Victoria Place is another road off West Hill. Probably the best known property in the past was Montpellier. First it was used as a girls' boarding school and then it became an hotel.

Budleigh Salterton, Westboro' Terrace.

Victoria Place, Budleigh Salterton.

(Above) Time for some refreshment! A horse enjoys a drink from the trough, or drinking fountain, which stood in West Hill and may have been responsible for the nearby cul-de-sac being called Fountain Hill.

(Top right) A horse-drawn cart makes a delivery to a house in East Terrace while a couple of girls show a keen interest in another one coming along the road. The sender of this card had come to spend Christmas 1923 in Budleigh Salterton.

(Bottom right) 'Residential tranquillity' would seem an apt title for this card showing West Terrace in Edwardian times.

Budleigh Salterton, East Terrace.

Budleigh Salterton, West Terrace.

(Above) Once part of Moor Lane, this stretch of road was re-christened Station Road shortly before this card was published. The obvious reason for this was the arrival of the railway to Budleigh Salterton.

(Opposite top) The railway branch from Exmouth to Tipton St John and on to Sidmouth Junction (Feniton) ran through Budleigh Salterton for nearly 64 years but was a victim of 'The Beeching Axe'; the last train ran on 4 March 1967. This postcard, believed to date back to the 1920s, shows passengers waiting for a train to arrive on the 'up' platform. The photograph was taken from the station footbridge.

(Opposite bottom) Some people preferred to come to Budleigh Salterton not by train, but by boat. Paddle steamers, like the *Duke* and *Duchess of Devonshire*, were frequent visitors to the town and boarding or disembarking meant 'walking the plank' between boat and beach. This particular card was published locally by F. W. Dalgleish of The Library, Budleigh Salterton.

MUSIC

BUDLEIGH SALTERTON - LOOKING EAST.

This fine photograph goes back to the times when the distinctive line of trees, which cap the low river cliff beside the Otter, were just young trees. This delightful rural scene is from the camera of local photographer F. T. Blackburn

and shows harvesting in progress in the field overlooking the mouth of the estuary. Beyond it the present large car park has yet to be constructed. To the north of that the fields in the picture are now developed.

F. T. Blackburn, the photographer, was obviously a man of enterprise. In August 1910, after a severe storm caused damage to the boats on the beach, he was out and about to record the scene above. Then he turned them into souvenir postcards.

The more usual view below was on a postcard sent in August 1939. As the storm clouds of war gathered over Europe, this card bore the message, "I am spending the day at Budleigh Salterton, one of my favourite spots."

Opposite is the Temple Methodist Church in Fore Street, built in 1905 on the site of a former church that dated from 1812. The wag sending the card, in the 1920s, decided to bestow on it the title of 'The Town Clock'.

Overleaf is a double page view of Budleigh Salterton's beach as it looked at the time of the First World War.

The Town Clock
Budleigh Salterton,
Wesleyan Methodist Church

BUDLEIGH SALTERTON.

"How do you manage to concentrate on the game?" is what a non-golfer might ask, bearing in mind the superb views to be enjoyed from the golf club on the cliffs to the west of the town. Maybe the sender of this card, in 1917, was spending his time in the Club House, and not out on the course, as he wrote, "Am enjoying myself and my thumb is getting better."

On the opposite page are two views of the annual carnival, a highlight of the year in days gone by. These pre-First World War postcards capture the atmosphere of the event – a barrel organ outside The Feathers Hotel and a group of mounted and walking entries in front of The Rolle Hotel.

POSTING

Above we have a street scene in East Budleigh taken in 1907. The travelling salesman was a welcome sight for villagers with his well-laden cart.

Opposite is a postcard that records the local connection with Sir Walter Raleigh. The Octagon in Salterton is where the artist Millais painted his 'Boyhood of Raleigh'.

Below are the lads of East Budleigh as they looked all those years ago when posing for a photo at Drake's School.

Budleigh Salterton, "The Octago
House where Millais painted
"Boyhood of Raleigh".

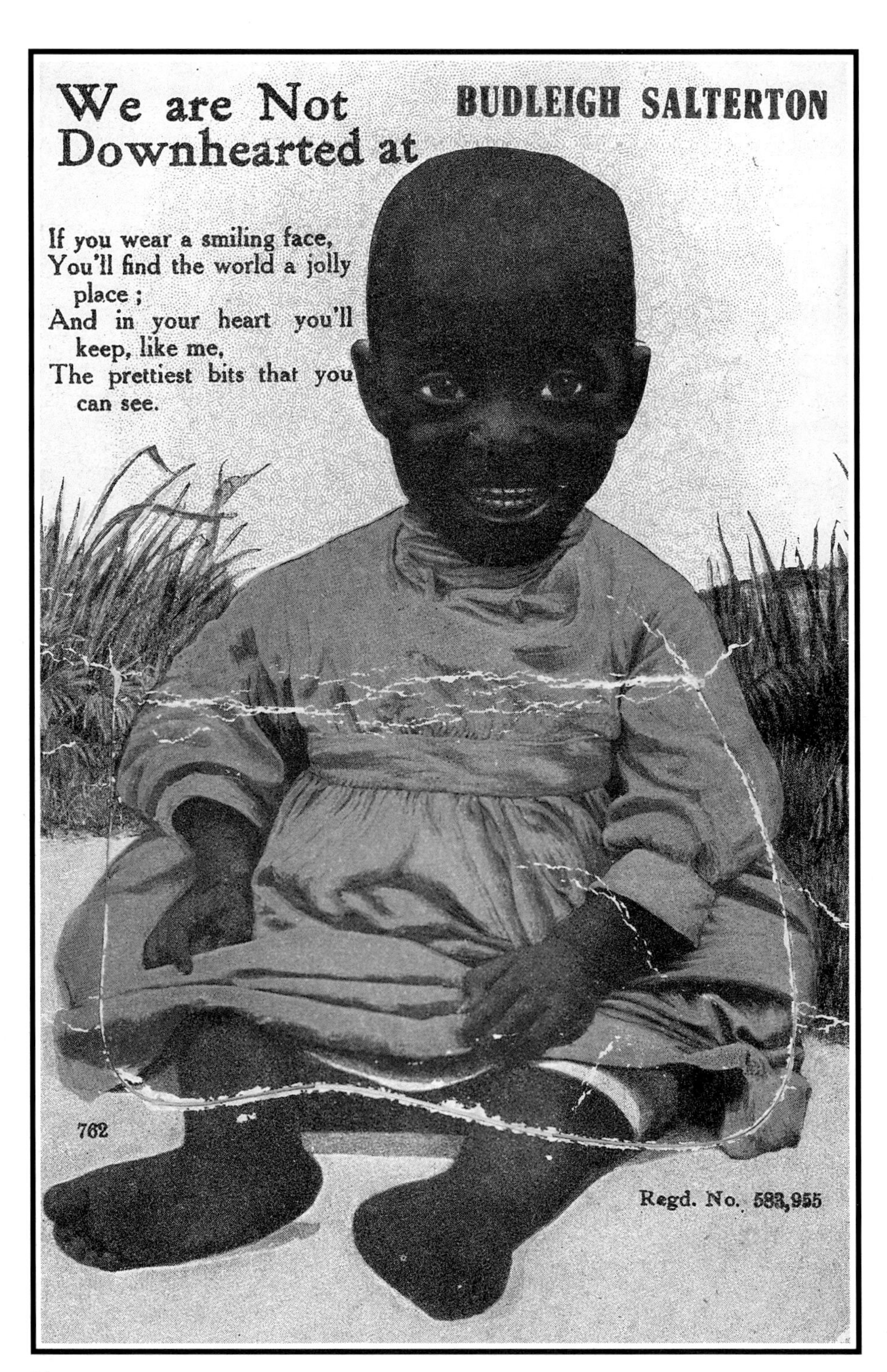
We are Not Downhearted at
BUDLEIGH SALTERTON
If you wear a smiling face,
You'll find the world a jolly place ;
And in your heart you'll keep, like me,
The prettiest bits that you can see.
762
Regd. No. 583,955

Two very different postcards! One is the standard view card at Shortwood whilst the other is a novelty card that contained a flap on the front. This could be lifted to reveal a strip of twelve views. There were eight of Budleigh Salterton, and one each of East Budleigh, Otterton, Ladram Bay and Exmouth. This card was postmarked in August 1919 and was sent by 'Amy' to a friend in Exeter.

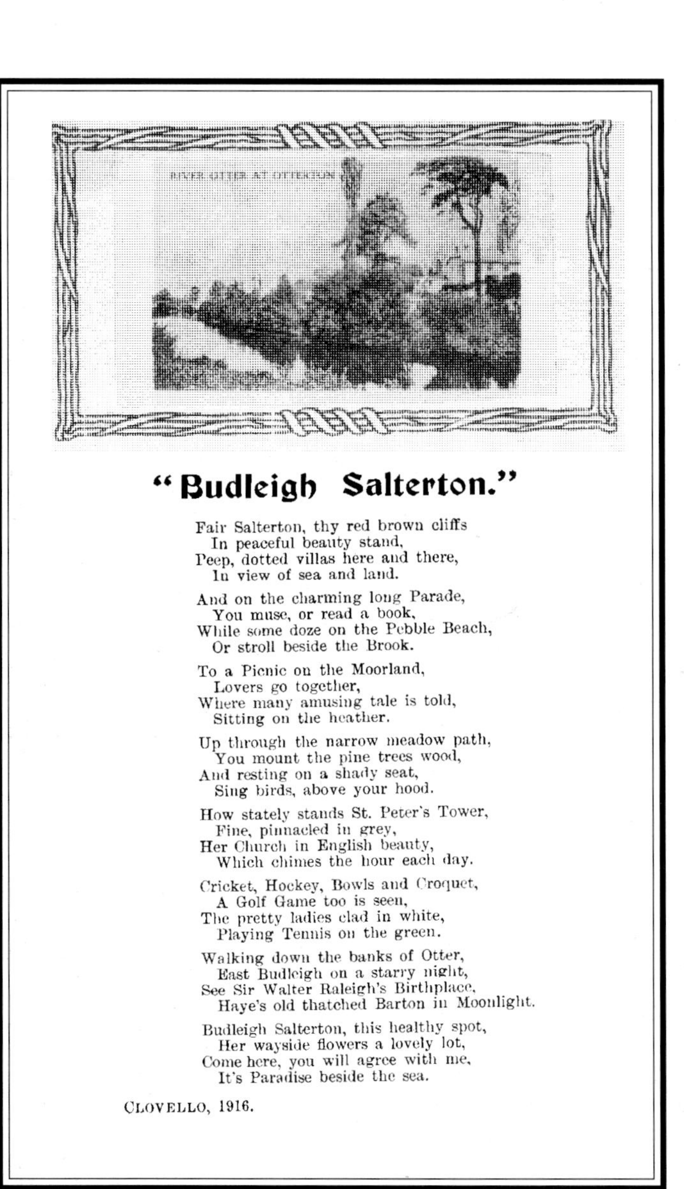

"Budleigh Salterton."

Fair Salterton, thy red brown cliffs
In peaceful beauty stand,
Peep, dotted villas here and there,
In view of sea and land.

And on the charming long Parade,
You muse, or read a book,
While some doze on the Pebble Beach,
Or stroll beside the Brook.

To a Picnic on the Moorland,
Lovers go together,
Where many amusing tale is told,
Sitting on the heather.

Up through the narrow meadow path,
You mount the pine trees wood,
And resting on a shady seat,
Sing birds, above your hood.

How stately stands St. Peter's Tower,
Fine, pinnacled in grey,
Her Church in English beauty,
Which chimes the hour each day.

Cricket, Hockey, Bowls and Croquet,
A Golf Game too is seen,
The pretty ladies clad in white,
Playing Tennis on the green.

Walking down the banks of Otter,
East Budleigh on a starry night,
See Sir Walter Raleigh's Birthplace,
Haye's old thatched Barton in Moonlight.

Budleigh Salterton, this healthy spot,
Her wayside flowers a lovely lot,
Come here, you will agree with me,
It's Paradise beside the sea.

CLOVELLO, 1916.

Above is a postcard sent to First World War soldiers and sailors as a reminder of their home town.

(Opposite top) Long before the days of such soccer jargon as 'strikers', 'substitutes' and 'professional fouls' it was quite an occasion for a village team to pose for a photo. This 'shot' became a postcard and shows the fine body of sportsmen who played as the 1911/12 Otterton & Bicton FC.

(Opposite bottom) 'Under the spreading chestnut tree' is Otterton Village as captured by our friend F. T. Blackburn.

OTTERTON & BICTON FOOTBALL TEAM. 1911-12.

Not far away is Ladram Bay but beware the trickery of the postcard publisher! First a photograph would be taken of a place then the details, like the people and boats, would be added later in the studio to give 'life' to the scene.

Below is a 1920s view of Knowle Village on the outskirts of Salterton.

The now much-used road across Woodbury Common was little more than a track when this horse-drawn vehicle made its way along it. The earthwork, known as Woodbury Castle, is said to date from the Iron Age and bore the name of Alauna Sylva.

The Common is no stranger to troops who have trained here for decades. This picture of 1917 was taken at their camp. Here they are gathered for a Church Parade and the photographer was on hand to ensure that postcards could be made for the men to send to their loved ones at home.

With so much nostalgia around we end our trip through time with a refreshing cup of tea, but which of these two charming tea-rooms would we have chosen? (Above) The Bungalow Tea Rooms on Woodbury Common proved a popular place to stop for tea when on a trip out into the country. Below are the premises, in Woodbury, of J. Hall, possibly seen here with his good lady, ready to serve you a truly scrumptious tea… we'll certainly drink to that!